Wrinkle-Faced Bats

ABDO
Publishing Company

A Buddy Book

by
Julie Murray

VISIT US AT
www.abdopub.com

Published by Buddy Books, an imprint of ABDO Publishing Company, 4940 Viking Drive, Suite 622, Edina, Minnesota 55435.

Printed in the United States.

Edited by: Christy DeVillier
Contributing Editors: Matt Ray, Michael P. Goecke
Graphic Design: Maria Hosley
Image Research: Deborah Coldiron
Cover Photograph: Bat Conservation International
Interior Photographs: Digial Stock, Denise Esner, Desmond Layne, Jeremy Miller, Photodisc

Library of Congress Cataloging-in-Publication Data

Murray, Julie, 1969-
Wrinkle-faced bats/Julie Murray.
p. cm. — (Animal kingdom)
Summary: An introduction to the physical characteristics, behavior, and habitat of the wrinkle-faced bat, a small mammal with wings.
ISBN 1-57765-710-1
1. Wrinkle-faced bat—Juvenile literature. [1. Wrinkle-faced bat. 2. Bats.] I. Title. II. Animal kingdom (Edina, Minn.)

QL737.C57 M87 2002
599.4'5—dc21

2001053873

Contents

Bats

Bats have been around for almost 50 million years. Bats are the only **mammals** that can fly.

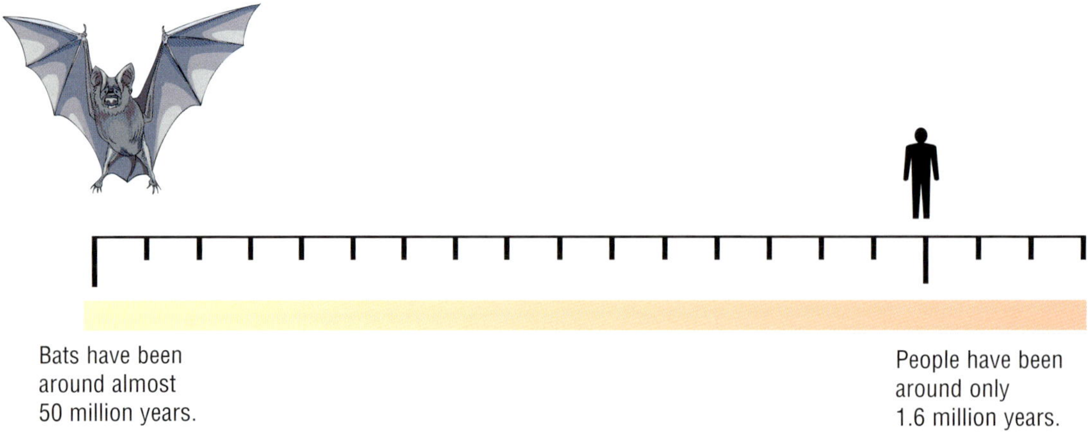

Different kinds of bats look different from each other.

There are more than 900 kinds of bats. Wrinkle-faced bats live in Mexico, Central America, and South America. They favor forests and open areas. Wrinkle-faced bats will **roost** in mango and rayo trees. They may live together in small groups of two or three.

Kinds Of Bats

There are two main groups of bats: megabats and microbats. Megabats are called fruit bats. Many kinds of megabats only eat fruit. Megabats have big eyes and good eyesight. They live in warm places in Asia, Africa, and Australia.

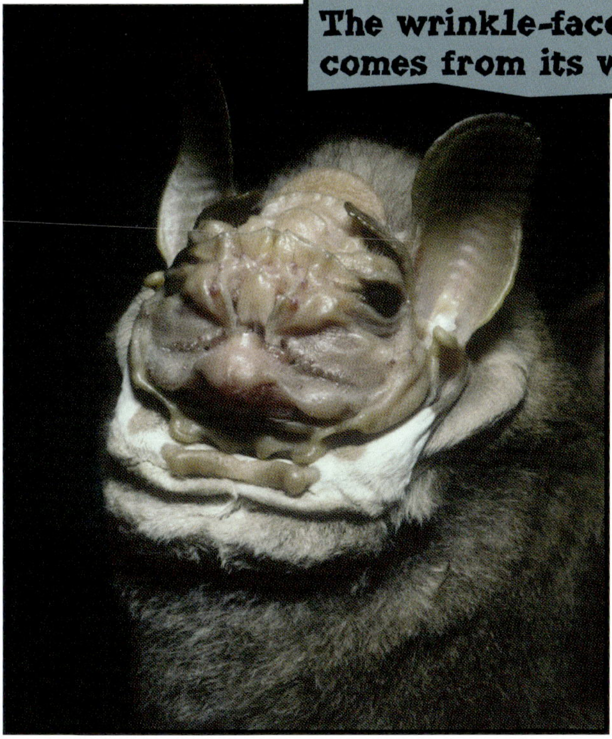

The wrinkle-faced bat's name comes from its wrinkled face.

The wrinkle-faced bat is a microbat. Most microbats are smaller than megabats. They have small eyes and big ears. Their wings are good for flying fast. Most microbats eat insects. Some of these bats also eat fruit.

What They Look Like

The wrinkle-faced bat has a round head and a hairless, wrinkled face. Its chin has a loose piece of skin that stretches. This skin can stretch over the bat's mouth and eyes.

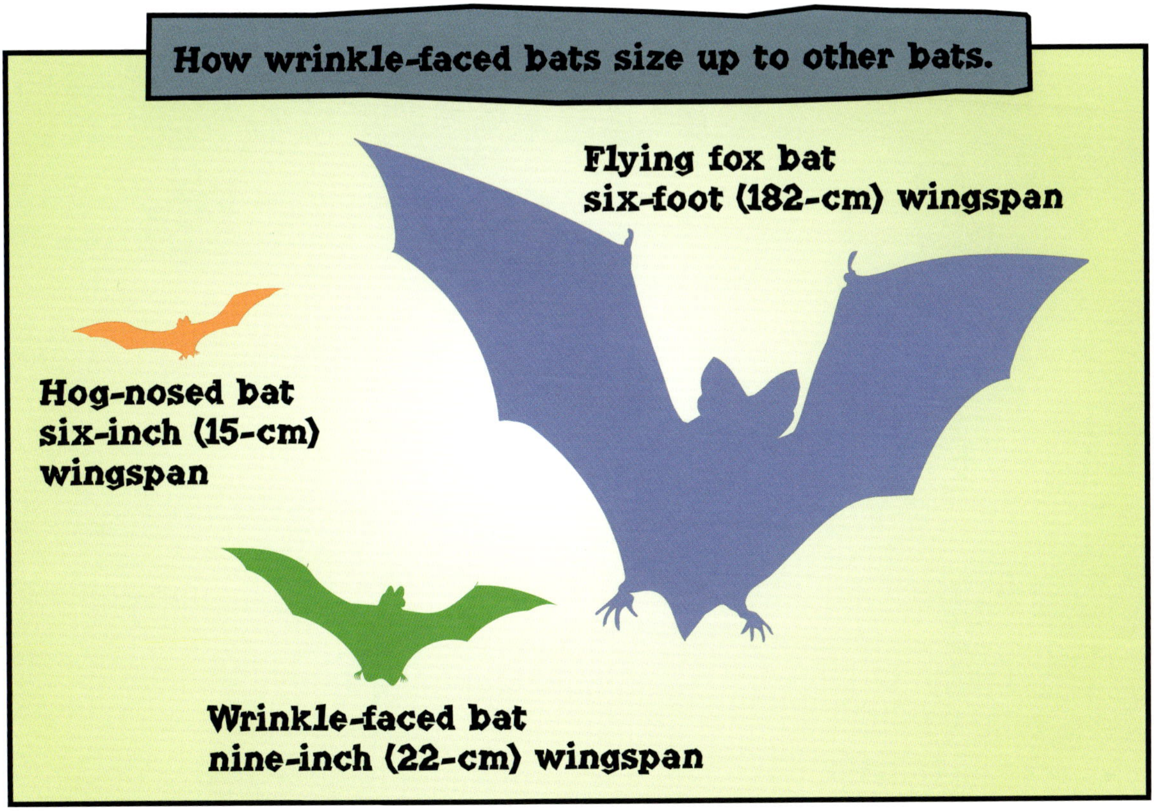

Wrinkle-faced bats weigh about one ounce (28 g). They grow to become about two inches (50 mm) tall.

Bat Wings

Bats are the only **mammals** that have wings. A bat's wings have two layers of skin. This skin stretches tightly over a bat's outspread wings.

There are four bones inside each wing of a wrinkle-faced bat. These bones are a bat's fingers. Bats also have a fifth finger, or thumb. A claw is on each thumb.

A bat has four bones inside each of its wings.

Skin stretches tightly over a bat's outstretched wings.

Roosting

Bats sleep, or **roost**, during the day. They may roost in trees, barns, caves, or attics. A roosting place may have a few bats or thousands.

Wrinkle-faced bats roost upside down. They hang by their toe claws. A roosting bat often covers itself with its wings.

Wrinkle-faced bats hang upside down to roost.

Eating

Bats eat a lot of different foods. They will eat insects, fruit, fish, frogs, birds, and **pollen**. Wrinkle-faced bats mostly eat fruit. They favor soft fruits like bananas and **papaws**.

Wrinkle-faced bats eat papaws.

Insects, frogs, and birds are food for bats, too.

Bats Are Helpful

Many kinds of bats eat grasshoppers, beetles, and moths. These insects eat farm crops. Bats help farmers by eating these harmful pests.

Bats eat mosquitoes, too. Some people keep bats nearby to kill mosquitoes.

Bats eat insect pests that kill farm crops.

Echolocation

Bats can see. But bats use sounds to find their way, too. They will make sounds, then listen to the echoes. The echoes tell them the size and shape of what is ahead. This is called **echolocation**. Echolocation helps bats find food, too.

Bats use echolocation to find food.

Bat Pups

Baby bats are called **pups**. A newborn bat pup is helpless. It needs its mother for milk and safety. Milk helps a bat pup to grow fast. Once it is three weeks old, it can fly.

Bat pups need their mother.

Important Words

echolocation using sounds and echoes to learn the shape and size of objects ahead.

mammal most living things that belong to this special group have hair, give birth to live babies, and make milk to feed their babies.

papaw the yellow fruit of a North American tree with purple flowers.

pollen the tiny, yellow grains of flowers.

pup a baby bat.

roost to rest or sleep. Bats roost during the day.

Web Sites

bats4kids

http://members.aol.com/bats4kids
Visit a bat cave and take a bat quiz.

Echo the Bat

http://imagers.gsfc.nasa.gov/intro/story.html
Learn more about bats by reading the story, "Echo the Bat."

Bats

www.cccoe.k12.ca.us/bats/know.html
More information on bats can be found here.

Index